Dismissing Senior Executives

By Daniel Barnett
and Francesca Read

The Employment Law Library

All books in the Employment Law Library are sent for free to members of the HR Inner Circle.

1. Employee Investigations
2. GDPR for HR Professionals
3. Preventing and Defending Employee Stress Claims
4. Employment Tribunal Time Limits
5. Deconstructing TUPE
6. Changing Terms & Conditions
7. Constructive Dismissal
8. Resolving Grievances
9. HR Hazards
10. Employment Status
11. Spotting Malingering
12. Employment Tribunal Compensation
13. Hiring Staff
14. Computer and Social Media Misuse
15. Managing Sickness Absence
16. The Three Ps
17. Conflict at Work
18. SOSR Dismissals
19. Dismissing Problem Employees
20. Menopause and the Workplace
21. Dismissing Senior Executives
22. Negotiating Exit Packages and Settlement Agreements

Published by HR Inner Circle Limited, Unit 3, Chequers Farm, Chequers Lane, Watford, Hertfordshire WD25 0LG

ISBN 978-1-918091-00-7

Acknowledgments

Welcome to book 21 in this series of mini guides on employment law for HR professionals.

Thanks to Tincuta Collett for the layout and design, Aaron Gaff for proofreading, and Maria Rodriguez for converting the book into the formats needed for Amazon.

Francesca Read would also like to thank her family for their support when writing this book, Daniel Barnett for the opportunity to collaborate and Jennie Hargrove for her help and encouragement.

None of these books are possible without the input and experience of the members of the HR Inner Circle. We write these small books for you, and you get them for free as part of your membership.

If you're not a member of the HR Inner Circle and you're interested in learning more about membership (www.hrinnercircle.co.uk), there is some information at the back of this book.

Daniel Barnett
Francesca Read

DANIEL BARNETT
BARRISTER
SUBSCRIBE
HOME
COMMUNITY
CHANNELS
ABOUT
HELP I'M BEING BULLIED AT WORK
Help - I'm being bullied at work: a practical guide for...
The most heartbreaking, emotional call I've ever take...
HOW TO HANDLE DISCIPLINARY, DISMISSAL AND PERFORMANCE MANAGEMENT
How to Handle Disciplinary, Dismissal and Performance...
ASK THE PRESIDENT
FAIRNESS IN REDUNDANCY SELECTION
Fair Redundancy Dismissals with Rebecca Tuck QC
THE UK'S LEADING YOUTUBE CHANNEL FOR LAW EXPLAINER VIDEOS
WWW.YOUTUBELEGAL.CO.UK

About the Authors

Daniel Barnett is an employment law barrister, practising from Chambers in London. He is the founder of the HR Inner Circle, is one of the UK's leading trainers on employment law, and presents the Legal Hour on LBC Radio.

Francesca Read is an employment lawyer with over 20 years' experience gained in both private practice and professional support roles. She works alongside Daniel and the team at HR Inner Circle, providing employment law support, insight and expertise.

Contents

Chapter 1
Introduction

A dismissal is a dismissal. The nuts and bolts are the same regardless of the identity of the employee in question. The law on unfair dismissal is not applied any differently to a CEO than it is to a shop worker. However, where the employee is a senior executive, the surrounding circumstances are often more complex, and the stakes are usually higher. This book aims to provide HR professionals with a comprehensive overview of the challenges that come with dismissing those holding senior positions, as well as the tools to address them.

While this book touches on how to carry out a fair dismissal of a senior executive, the overall focus is on the broader challenges involved in making that happen.

There are three key areas of risk:

1. **Legal** – This includes the risk of claims arising from the dismissal itself, including unfair dismissal, discrimination or whistleblowing – all of which can be high-value and reputationally damaging.

2. **Financial** – The cost of exit often goes beyond salary and notice, including bonus entitlements, share schemes and long-term incentives, as well as the potential cost of defending or settling any claims.

3. **Commercial** – Senior executives often have deep knowledge of the business, client relationships and

access to sensitive commercial information. A poorly handled exit can damage internal morale and disrupt investor or client confidence. There is also the risk of reputational damage to the business.

This book is HRs practical companion, taking you through the challenges and pitfalls to demonstrate how to dismiss a senior executive effectively.

Chapter 2
Why it's important to do your homework

It's important not to jump headfirst into a process when seeking to dismiss a senior executive. There are some circumstances in which you can, for example, a clear act of gross misconduct or an identified redundancy situation. These are covered in chapters 9 and 10. But such circumstances are relatively rare. More commonly, a senior exit is driven by commercial or strategic considerations; perhaps the business wants to shift direction, there has been a breakdown in trust, or the executive is simply no longer seen as the right fit. These types of situations often do not map neatly onto the 'potentially fair reasons' for dismissal set out in the *Employment Rights Act 1996*.

You need to take time to consider who you are dealing with. Senior executives often have complex contractual arrangements that go beyond the basics of salary and notice periods. Their packages may include long-term incentive plans, share options, bonus schemes, enhanced pension rights and post-termination restrictions. Dismissing them without fully reviewing their contractual entitlements and potential claims can significantly increase financial and reputational risk.

A senior figure may hold confidential information, valuable client connections or influence within the organisation.

Mishandling their departure could create disruption, internal instability or even external reputational fallout.

It's vital that HR professionals step back, gather the facts, assess the legal position, review the financial exposure and understand the personalities involved. Think ahead: what are the legal justifications? What are the commercial consequences? Who else needs to be consulted? Only once you have mapped the risks and options can you confidently proceed – whether that's starting a process, proposing an exit negotiation or seeking advice.

Doing your homework beforehand could save you a lot of trouble later.

Over the next five chapters, this book demonstrates how you can, slowly and carefully, work out exactly who you are dealing with.

Chapter 3

Who is this person?

Senior executives often wear more than one 'hat' within a business. In other words, they may hold several roles or legal statuses. Before starting any dismissal process, it's crucial to identify exactly what those roles are and how they affect the process.

Are they an 'employee'?

This should be one of the first things you confirm. In most cases, a senior executive will be an employee. An employee typically works under a contract of employment, is paid for their work and is subject to the employer's control over how, when and where they work.

Check your records for an employment contract or director's service agreement. Gather all relevant documents, including any bonus, commission or incentive schemes tied to their role.

Are they a statutory director?

Many senior executives have the title 'Director', but not all are statutory directors – that is, formally registered as directors at Companies House. The title may just reflect their job role, not a legal office.

Statutory directors have fiduciary duties to act in the best interests of the company, including duties of loyalty and honesty. These duties (and breaches of them) can support conduct or capability allegations if you're considering dismissal.

Ending someone's employment does not remove them as a statutory director. Check the service agreement early to see if it includes terms that require resignation as a director when employment ends.

In most cases, executives will resign directorships once a settlement is agreed. Always ensure you get written confirmation of resignation, ideally as part of a settlement agreement.

If the executive refuses to resign, consider:

- **Articles of Association** – Do they automatically remove directors when employment ends? It's rare that they do, but worth checking.
- **Service agreement** – Does it require the executive to resign from all group roles? Some agreements include a power of attorney allowing the company to sign resignation letters. For this to be valid, the contract must have been signed as a deed.
- **Statutory removal** – If no other option is available, you can remove a director via a shareholder vote under sections 168 and 169 of the *Companies Act 2006*. This requires an ordinary resolution (over 50% approval) with 28 days' notice.

Are you offering a statutory director a settlement sum?

If you're offering a settlement to a statutory director, consider the rules on payments for loss of office. Most payments made in good faith – such as contractual payments, damages or pensions – don't need shareholder approval under sections 220 and 221 of the *Companies Act 2006*. But if the payment doesn't clearly fall into these categories, shareholder approval may be required under section 217.

Do they hold any group company roles?

If the executive is a statutory director of the employing company, they may also hold roles within other group companies. It is important, when mapping out a potential exit, to do your due diligence and uncover any 'group' roles that will also need to be terminated as part of the executive's exit. You can undertake a search of statutory roles held by inputting the executive's name here: https://find-and-update.company-information.service.gov.uk.

Are there any director loan agreements in place?

When the executive is a director, it is important to check whether they have made any loans to the company (or vice versa) that remain outstanding. It is important to consider the repayment terms of any loans and the extent to which the loans are affected by their departure from the business.

Loans owed by the director to the company can be a useful bargaining chip in negotiations. The company could offer to write the loan off as part of a settlement deal. The amount written off is treated as a deemed dividend under the *Income Tax (Trading and Other Income) Act 2005*. Because it is a deemed dividend, there is no requirement for the company to have available profits for distribution, and the dividend does not need to be paid to all shareholders of a particular class of shares. However, an important feature of a loan being written off is that in most cases, HMRC will argue that writing off a loan comes under the definition of 'emoluments from an office or employment' and, as a result, will seek to collect Class 1 NICs from the company. This is an additional cost to the business, which should be borne in mind.

Remuneration policy and directors' remuneration reports

Where the departing executive is a statutory director, the business needs to be aware of the potential impact of the business's remuneration policy. For listed companies, payments for loss of office must often align with the company's forward-looking remuneration policy. If the proposed settlement falls outside of this framework, shareholder approval may be needed.

Are they a shareholder?

If the individual is a shareholder as well as a director, you will need to consider the impact of dismissal on that shareholding.

The senior executive may have a separate Shareholders' Agreement that will need to be considered. Again, as with employment, pull together all documents and be ready to take specialist advice. This is a corporate matter. There could be a clause that says a shareholding executive must automatically surrender any shares if they cease to be an employee, and this clause is likely to say how those shares must be valued. If there is no clause setting out the valuation of the shares, dismissal discussions will need to include how the shares should be valued.

Are they all three?

It is not unusual for a senior executive to wear all three of these hats: employee, statutory director and shareholder. If you are contemplating dismissing a senior executive, then each of these 'hats' will need to be considered carefully, both in terms of the process followed and the end-point reached.

Chapter 4
Understanding your business

Before you begin the process of dismissing a senior executive, take time to understand the wider business context. It's not enough to focus on their role or contract alone.

Senior executives rarely work in isolation. They often have influence across key areas – including customers, investors, staff and strategy. Removing them without considering this broader picture can lead to disruption and unintended risks.

The following are key points to consider.

1. What kind of business is it?

Start by understanding the type of business you're dealing with. Is it built around intellectual property, such as in tech, media or pharma? If so, check what protections are in place. That includes IP clauses, confidentiality terms and post-termination restrictions in the employment contract.

Is the business in a fast-moving or competitive industry? If yes, a departing executive could pose a real risk. They may take sensitive knowledge or clients with them unless properly restricted.

2. How visible is the executive?

Some executives are the face of the business. If they manage key customer relationships, their exit could harm contracts or reputation. In this case, consider garden leave – where the executive remains employed during notice but is kept away from day-to-day work. Make sure the contract allows for this.

Also, think about the internal impact. Does this person lead a loyal team? Could their departure cause others to leave too? If so, check whether their contract includes a non-poaching clause to help protect the business (see Chapter 7 for more on this).

Knowing how much influence the executive holds – both inside and outside the company – can help you plan for a smooth transition.

3. Are there disclosure duties?

If the company is listed, dismissal of a senior executive who is also a statutory director may trigger disclosure requirements under the UK Listing Rules or Market Abuse Regulation. You'll need to check whether an announcement is required and if so, when and how it should be made. If the company is a 'quoted' company (either on FTSE, NYSE, NASDAQ or in an EEA state), the Listing Rules require notification to a Regulatory Information Service of the removal of a director by no later than the end of the business day following the decision, stating when the removal will take effect. AIM companies are not quoted companies.

For all executive exits, Form TM01 should be filed at Companies House within 14 days of the termination of the director's directorship. The company will also need to update its register of directors and register of directors' residential addresses to reflect the change.

4. Is the business regulated?

If the organisation is in a regulated sector (e.g. financial services, education, healthcare or law), the executive's departure may need to be reported to a regulatory authority.

In sectors such as financial services, healthcare, education and law, there may be a requirement to notify the relevant regulator when a senior executive leaves their role, especially if the departure is connected to misconduct or concerns over their fitness to practice.

- **Financial services** (e.g. Financial Conduct Authority (FCA)/Prudential Regulation Authority (PRA)-regulated firms) – If the executive is a Senior Manager Function (SMF) holder or Certified Person under the Senior Managers and Certification Regime (SMCR), you may need to:
    - Submit a Form C (ceasing to perform a function).
    - Submit a Form D if there are any conduct rule breaches or concerns.
    - Consider Statements of Responsibilities and regulatory references.
    - Maintain accurate records of conduct in the event of a future FCA inquiry.
- **Healthcare** – You may need to inform the Care Quality Commission if a registered manager or senior individual departs or if concerns arise relating to patient safety or regulatory compliance. If the individual is a doctor, then the General Medical Council may need to

be informed if the termination is due to misconduct or other reasons that could affect fitness to practice.

- **Education and law sectors** – Senior departures involving misconduct or regulatory breaches may need to be reported to Ofsted, the Solicitors Regulatory Authority or the Bar Standards Board, depending on the setting.

Some regulators impose strict deadlines for notification (e.g. FCA forms must usually be submitted within seven business days). Failing to notify promptly can result in enforcement action or reputational damage.

Summary

By stepping back and considering the business as a whole, HR professionals can come up with a clear plan of action covering each area, identify which internal teams (e.g. legal, compliance, investor relations) need to be involved, and help shape an exit strategy that protects the company and meets its wider responsibilities.

Chapter 5

The employment contract: an introduction

The employment contract is the foundation of the relationship between the business and the senior executive. It's essential to locate and review all relevant contractual documents at the start of any potential dismissal or exit process.

The document may be called a 'Contract of Employment' or a 'Director's Service Agreement'. The name doesn't matter – what's important is what it says.

Is it the current contract?

Once you find the contract, check it's up to date and valid. Is it signed? Was it sent with a covering letter? Has it been updated following role changes or pay rises?

You want to avoid a situation where the executive claims the contract was never finalised or isn't binding.

Key clauses to focus on

Senior executive contracts are often long and detailed. Don't get lost in every word. Instead, focus on the parts that matter most for planning an exit. These will shape the process, the legal risks and what you can negotiate.

The chapters that follow focus in detail on some of the most commercially important provisions that you'll want to review closely:

- **Notice provisions, payment in lieu of notice (PILON) and garden leave** – These determine how quickly you can bring the employment to an end, whether you have the right to pay the executive in lieu of working their notice period (and the basis upon which any such payment should be made), and whether you can require them to stay away from the business during that time (see Chapter 6).
- **Confidentiality, intellectual property and post–termination restrictions** – These clauses protect your business during and after employment, particularly where a senior executive has access to sensitive information, client relationships or IP (see Chapter 7).

There are a number of other clauses that, while not covered in full chapters, are still worth flagging:

- **Summary termination / gross misconduct** – The relevance of these provisions will largely depend on the background to the business's proposal to dismiss. Most senior contracts include a list of examples of gross misconduct that justify immediate dismissal. No notice pay is payable if you can hang your hat on one of these. These lists are generally regarded as non-exhaustive. Just because an allegation isn't included in the list doesn't mean that it cannot be gross misconduct. However, if the allegation is on the list, then this can help with framing the allegation and demonstrating that the executive should have been aware that the misconduct was serious.

- **Probationary period** – This is mainly relevant if the executive is new. Probation clauses often allow for quicker, simpler dismissals – sometimes without using the formal disciplinary process. They may also set shorter notice periods, making dismissal less costly.

  Right now, unfair dismissal rights only apply after two years of service. But this will change in (probably) autumn 2026, when it becomes a day-one right. Until then, probation clauses can still make exits easier in the early stages.

- **Permanent Health Insurance (PHI)** – PHI is a benefit that provides salary (or a portion of it) if the executive can't work due to long-term illness. Payments can sometimes last until retirement. These schemes usually only pay out while the person is still officially employed.

  If you're considering dismissal while an executive is on PHI, tread carefully. Ending their contract might stop the insurance payments, exposing the business to legal risk. In *Aspden v Webbs Poultry [1996] IRLR 521*, the court ruled it was a breach of contract to dismiss someone just to avoid PHI payments. Damages can be high, possibly covering lost payments right through to retirement.

- **Suspension** – If a senior executive is facing allegations of potential gross misconduct, you should think early on about whether to suspend them during the investigation.

Most employment contracts include a suspension clause. This gives the employer the right to suspend the executive if gross misconduct is alleged. These clauses usually also explain how pay will be handled during the suspension.

Even if there's no suspension clause, you may still be able to suspend (on pay). An issue only generally arises where the role includes a strong right to work. This right only tends to apply where pay depends heavily on personal performance or where long periods away from work could harm the executive's skills.

If you do suspend, it should be made clear that this is a neutral act – not a punishment – and it should last no longer than necessary.

- **Company sick pay** – If the departure is likely to be contentious and the executive might look to make things difficult, then it is worth checking any contractual provisions relating to sick pay. If the executive has a right to full pay during sickness absence, then the business needs to be aware that the executive may tactically deploy sickness absence to disrupt the business at no financial cost to them.
- **Resignation from directorships** – The interplay between an executive's employed role and their role as a statutory director was covered in Chapter 3. In terms of reviewing the employment contract, if the executive

is a statutory director, check whether the contract requires them to resign as a director upon termination of employment. Some contracts also include a power of attorney clause, allowing the company to sign resignation documents on the executive's behalf if they refuse to cooperate. These clauses are vital if you want a clean and simple severance process.

- **Bonus, commission and incentive plans** – These often sit outside the main contract but can have major implications. You'll want to check the contract for any references and whether leavers forfeit rights or pro rata payments if an executive leaves part-way through a year, and whether there's discretion involved in making payments.
- **Expenses, loans and company property** – Check for any repayment clauses or obligations to return items, especially where there are outstanding advances, relocation loans or access to sensitive data. Senior executives often have use of company items, such as company cars and tech (including mobile phones and computers).
- **Deductions from final pay** – Look for a contractual right to make deductions from salary or bonus payments, for example, if the executive owes the business money.

Ultimately, contractual details matter. The right clause – or the absence of one – can dramatically shift the balance of power in a negotiation and impact the options available to the business.

Chapter 6

Notice, PILON and garden leave

When planning the departure of a senior executive, the fine print of their contract can make or break the strategy. Key clauses around notice, PILON and garden leave play a critical role in shaping both the timing and terms of an exit.

This chapter explores how these provisions operate in practice, the legal and tactical considerations they raise, and how they can be used to manage risk, protect business interests and ensure a smoother transition.

Notice

The service agreement usually includes an express notice clause. When considering the dismissal of a senior executive, you should look out for the following:

- **Any rules for how notice should be given** – Does it need to be given in writing to be effective? You want to make sure that when notice is given, it is effective. There should be no room for uncertainty.
- **The length of notice required to be given by the employer** – For senior executives, this is often six or, in some cases, 12 months. If a low notice period is stated in the contract, then make sure you check it

against the relevant statutory minimum. Statutory minimum notice periods are set out in section 86 of the *Employment Rights Act 1996* and provide that employees are entitled to receive at least one week's notice from their employer for each completed year of employment up to a maximum of 12 weeks after 12 years. If the contractual notice period is lower than the statutory notice period, then the statutory notice period will apply.

Pay in lieu of notice (PILON) clauses

PILON is a lump sum paid that is equal to the amount that the executive would have earned if they had continued in employment during their notice period. When contemplating the dismissal of a senior executive, consideration needs to be given as to whether there is a contractual right to pay in lieu of notice.

The starting point is to look at the contract of employment. If there is no PILON clause in the contract of employment, then you would technically breach the contract by making a PILON payment because you would remove the right of the executive to work. You could consider discussing the option with the executive, and you could use PILON if the executive agreed, but you would need to get this agreement confirmed in writing.

Making a PILON payment when there's no contractual right to do so can impact the enforceability of post-employment restrictions (e.g. restrictive covenants). An employer cannot rely on protections contained in an employment contract that they themselves have breached.

This means that post-employment restrictions and express confidentiality clauses would no longer apply.

If you do make a PILON payment in breach of contract, the payment will technically be damages for breach of contract. Therefore, when calculating this payment, you should include the cost of benefits (e.g. pension contributions, car allowance, holiday payments) in calculating the payment so that it fully represents the damages that have been incurred.

Things to look out for when reviewing a PILON clause:

- It should say that dismissal happens immediately when a payment is made in lieu of the (basic) salary that would have been earned during the notice period.
- It should identify what benefits and other payments (e.g. commissions, bonuses, pension contributions) are included and excluded from the PILON amount. Some PILON clauses state that only 'basic salary' is payable when an employer pays in lieu of notice. There is some sense in this. After all, the executive receives accelerated receipt of their salary and does not need to work for it. If the contractual PILON clause is silent as to what payments are included, full salary *plus* the value of any contractual benefits during the PILON period will be payable.
- It should explain how and when the payment will be made. Sometimes, PILON clauses state that payment will be made in instalments rather than as one lump sum. They can sometimes even include a mechanism whereby payments are reduced (or stopped entirely)

if the executive finds a new job whilst instalment payments remain outstanding.

An interesting question arises if an executive is put under notice, the employer exercises a PILON clause and then, at a later date, the employer discovers that the executive has done something which is gross misconduct. In *Williams v Leeds United Football Club [2015] EWHC 376* (in which one of the authors of this book represented Mr Williams!), the employee earned £200,000 a year working as a Technical Director of Leeds United. He was identified as being at risk of redundancy. After his notice period had started (but before any decision to pay in lieu of notice had been communicated), the Club discovered that he had sent a number of obscene emails to a junior female employee and two male friends. He was dismissed for gross misconduct. The employer argued, therefore, that summary dismissal was appropriate and no notice was payable.

This argument was upheld in the High Court. The employer had not entered into any agreement to pay in lieu of notice, and therefore, was not committed to do so. However, it is worth noting that the outcome would have been different if a PILON agreement had already been reached before the gross misconduct had been discovered. That is why it is always important that PILON is drafted as a discretionary *option* on termination that the employer may choose to take up (but is not obliged to).

It is important to be clear about the date of dismissal, as shown in *Societe Generale, London Branch v Geys [2012] UKSC 63*. Mr Geys was employed as Managing Director, and there was a clause in his employment contract that said either party could terminate the contract by giving three months' notice. It also said that if the bank terminated Mr Geys' employment, they had to pay him a compensation payment that was calculated based on the date when his employment was terminated. The staff handbook also contained a PILON clause that allowed the bank to terminate Mr Geys' employment by making a payment in lieu of notice.

Mr Geys was summarily dismissed on 29 November 2007, and on 18 December 2007, the bank paid into his bank account monies owed under the PILON clause. On 2 January 2008, Mr Geys' solicitors wrote to the bank to say that he was affirming his contract and wanted details of the termination payment. The bank then wrote to Mr Geys on 4 January 2008 to say that it had terminated his employment on 29 November and that he had been paid in accordance with the PILON clause.

Mr Geys brought claims for wrongful dismissal and breach of contract. He argued that his employment did not terminate until 6 January 2008, when he received the bank's letter, and this meant that his termination payment should have been €5.5million greater than the amount he had received, because of the calculation dates.

The Supreme Court ruled that, if an employer repudiates a contract of employment, the contract only ends when the employee accepts the repudiation. The contract does not end automatically when the repudiation occurs. Mr Geys' employment did not end until he had been clearly notified that the contract had come to an end, and it could not be argued that he had to check his bank account to see if his contract was still in place.

This case shows that the employer repudiating the contract of employment does not automatically end the contract. The employee can choose to affirm the contract or accept the repudiation. For the contract to end, there must be an acceptance of the repudiation.

Using PILON is attractive when terminating the employment of a senior executive because you are unlikely to want someone who is leaving to be actively working at a senior level in the organisation throughout their notice period.

Garden leave

An alternative to PILON is to place the executive on garden leave. This is when an executive remains on the payroll and all the obligations of the employer and the executive to each other remain, but the executive is instructed not to work.

The attraction of garden leave is that the duties of the executive to the employer (such as mutual trust and confidence) remain. If a senior executive has a reasonably long notice period (which would be common), there is no danger (as would exist with PILON) that the executive is working for a competitor. And by the time the contract ends and the executive perhaps moves on to work for a competitor, the executive's knowledge of what is happening in the business will be outdated, and the business will have had time to embed a successor.

Chapter 7

Confidentiality, IP and restrictive covenants

When considering the exit of a senior executive, it's important to review the provisions in place that might provide crucial protection for the business once the executive has left. Confidentiality, intellectual property and restrictive covenants are key to safeguarding the company's most valuable assets.

1. Confidentiality

A strong confidentiality clause makes it clear what the business believes constitutes confidential information. If no express confidentiality clause exists, then the senior executive's ongoing obligations following termination are limited to the protection of highly confidential information (akin to trade secrets) and are tricky to enforce. An express clause can protect much wider categories of information.

If there is no express confidentiality clause, then consider adding a detailed confidentiality clause into any settlement agreement. In order to be enforceable, it should be accompanied by a separate payment (which will be subject to tax and National Insurance deductions). This must be more than nominal – around £500 or £1,000 is common. It can, of course, come off the total settlement amount so as not to increase the overall amount paid.

2. Intellectual property

The importance of intellectual property (IP) provisions will depend on the executive's role and level of influence. A service agreement should state that any IP the executive creates while carrying out their duties belongs to the company, not the individual. This becomes critical on exit, as it stops the executive from claiming ownership of, or continuing to use, commercially valuable materials, products or ideas developed during their employment.

Agreements usually include a clause requiring the executive to transfer all rights in any invention to the company on request. If there are concerns that the executive might claim a previous discovery as their own, include an IP assignment clause in any settlement agreement. Also, consider whether there is a power of attorney clause allowing the company to sign the IP transfer on the executive's behalf if they refuse. A power of attorney is only valid if the employment contract was signed as a deed, so check this early on.

3. Restrictive covenants

Restrictive covenants (or, to give them their full title, post-termination restrictive covenants) are clauses in a senior executive's contract that limit what they can do after leaving the business. They're common, but how important they are depends on the role. If the executive is underperforming and not seen as a threat, restrictions may feel unnecessary. However, where the executive is customer-facing or has access to sensitive information, strong restrictive covenants can be vital.

There are three main types:

- **Non-compete** – This stops the executive working for a competitor.
- **Non-solicit** – This prevents them approaching your clients or suppliers (or, sometimes, staff).
- **Non-deal** – This prevents them working with your clients or suppliers, even if approached by them.

If the executive is also a shareholder, check any shareholder agreement early. Such agreements often include wider and more enforceable restrictions than employment contracts.

Covenants are generally unenforceable unless they are reasonable, protect a legitimate business interest and go no further than necessary to protect that interest. Courts look at:

- **Geographic scope** – Is it limited to where the executive worked?
- **Duration** – Is the length proportionate?
- **Activity** – Does it target specific risks, or is it too broad?

In *Bartholomews Agri Food Ltd v Thornton [2016] EWHC 648*, a six-month non-compete was unenforceable because it was imposed when the employee was junior and covered clients he had never dealt with.

Sometimes, if a covenant is too broad, the court may delete the offending part. In *Tillman v Egon Zehnder Ltd [2019] UKSC 32*, the words "or interested in" made a clause too wide, but the Supreme Court removed those words and upheld the rest.

The key is careful drafting. Overly broad restrictions won't be enforced, and vague covenants carry risk. Review them before a senior executive exits to understand your real level of protection.

Protecting the enforceability of restrictive covenants

If restrictive covenants are important in a senior executive's exit, it's vital that the employer doesn't act in a way that risks making them unenforceable. A breach of contract by the employer – such as failing to pay correctly, mishandling the dismissal process or acting in a way that undermines trust and confidence – can prevent the business from being able to rely on these provisions. The restrictive covenants may no longer bind the executive, because the courts can say, "If the employer doesn't follow the contract, why should we force the employee to?"

To preserve your position:

- Avoid breaching the contract in how you manage the dismissal.
- Don't suspend unreasonably, withhold pay, or handle the exit in a heavy-handed way.

Include covenants in any settlement agreement

Where a financial settlement is agreed, it's best practice to set out the restrictive covenants in the settlement agreement for a second time (having appeared first in the original employment contract).

If there's any doubt about whether the original clauses are enforceable, or if the exit process may have undermined them, you can amend and restate the covenant – as long as the executive receives something of value in return. Any additional consideration payment must be made subject to tax deductions, as it is a payment emanating from a contractual obligation.

This approach gives the employer a clearer legal footing if they later need to enforce the restrictions, and it removes any ambiguity about what the executive has agreed to on exit.

Chapter 8
Unfair dismissal: an introduction

The *Employment Rights Act 1996* contains the legal protection for employees against being unfairly dismissed.

The law on unfair dismissal is sometimes overlooked when managing the exits of senior executives. This is usually because of the financial complexity of director-level remuneration packages and the headline value of most senior settlements. With big figures in play – including share awards, bonuses and long-term incentives – compensation for unfair dismissal (which is generally capped – see below) can seem irrelevant.

But this is a mistake. The potential value of an unfair dismissal claim can still be used to frame the negotiation. An unfair dismissal finding might be the difference between someone being a 'good leaver' or a 'bad leaver'. It is also important for the business to consider what its 'open' position is on the dismissal if a deal falls through or discussions break down – is there a fair reason to fall back on?

Eligibility to claim: the two-year rule (for now)

To bring a claim for ordinary unfair dismissal, the employee must have at least two years' continuous employment. Importantly, this includes an extra statutory week, even if not actually worked. For example, if an employee has one year and 51 weeks' service, you must still add one week – meaning they may actually qualify to claim.

But this is set to change. Under the Employment Rights Bill (probably the *Employment Rights Act 2025* by the time of publication), unfair dismissal protection will become an effective 'day one right'. This is expected to come into force sometime in or after autumn 2026.

What makes a dismissal 'fair'?

To defend an unfair dismissal claim, an employer must show two things:

1. A potentially fair reason for dismissal.
2. That the dismissal was reasonable in all the circumstances.

The five potentially fair reasons are:

1. Conduct – For example, serious misconduct or breaches of trust.
2. Capability – For example, poor performance or health issues affecting the employee's ability to do the job.
3. Redundancy – Situations in which the role is no longer required.
4. Illegality – Situations in which continued employment would break the law.

5. Some other substantial reason – A broad category that can include loss of trust, breakdown of working relationships or business restructures.

Once a potentially fair reason is established, the tribunal will assess whether the employer acted reasonably. This means looking at the process followed, the evidence relied upon and whether the decision fell within the range of reasonable responses open to a reasonable employer.

Compensation for unfair dismissal

Compensation for unfair dismissal is made up of:

- A basic award (calculated in the same way as statutory redundancy pay – based on age, salary and years of service. A calculation can be carried out using this calculator: https://www.gov.uk/calculate-your-redundancy-pay).
- A compensatory award (covering financial losses, such as lost earnings and benefits).

As of April 2025, the maximum compensatory award is £118,223 or 12 months' gross pay, whichever is lower. The maximum increases by inflation each April. But for certain dismissals (e.g. whistleblowing or health and safety-related dismissals), this cap is removed, meaning awards can be uncapped and run into six or even seven figures. Unfair dismissal compensation is directly linked to the losses flowing from a dismissal. Employers should consider the likelihood that the executive will secure a new job, and when that is likely to happen. This can all influence settlement discussions.

Why unfair dismissal matters

For senior exits, especially where there's no clear case for misconduct or redundancy, an unfair dismissal claim may be a real risk – even if unlikely to reach tribunal. Understanding the rules provides a valuable negotiation framework and helps HR and legal teams shape a fair process that will stand up to scrutiny or justify the need for a settlement.

The next three chapters explore fair dismissal for conduct, capability and redundancy in further detail.

Chapter 9
An exploration of fair dismissal: gross misconduct

A lot of senior executive dismissals don't involve formal processes. The board will decide to dismiss the executive, and will put a package on the table. Getting the executive out quickly is generally regarded as a preferable option to keeping them in the business while going through any formal process.

But this is not always the case. If serious misconduct allegations have been made against the executive, then the business may see it as important that these allegations are investigated openly and transparently. We have all seen the adverse consequences for businesses where apparent wrongdoing is 'rewarded' with an agreed exit – think of recent examples such as Huw Edwards at the BBC and Tony Danker at CBI. The business's reputation can be undermined if an open process is abandoned when the allegations are serious.

If your senior executive stands accused of a serious misconduct allegation, then this is generally worth a closer look. An open process to dismissal may be warranted. At the very least, the senior executive's exit should be positioned with the allegation at the forefront.

One key reason is that if an allegation of gross misconduct is well founded, it can justify summary termination of employment – without any payment of notice pay. The value of a notice pay payment to a departing senior executive is often substantial. A finding of gross misconduct can also have a knock-on effect on other benefits the senior executive might have by classifying him as a 'bad leaver' for the purposes of any shares held and any long-term incentive plan in operation.

Whether you ever get that far with any open process is largely irrelevant. Once the executive knows that it is a genuine risk, it completely changes the dynamic at the negotiating table.

Gross misconduct

Whether it is reasonable for an employer to dismiss an executive for a conduct reason requires consideration of the classic 'Burchell test' set out in *British Home Stores v Burchell [1980] ICR 303*: whether, at the time of dismissal, the employer believed the executive to be guilty of misconduct, had reasonable grounds for believing that the executive was guilty of that misconduct and had carried out as much investigation as was reasonable in the circumstances. In any open process, a detailed investigation is key. The *Acas Code of Practice* on disciplinary and grievance procedures should be followed in any disciplinary or performance management situation.

The key principles are:

- Employers and employees should raise and deal with issues promptly and should not unreasonably delay meetings, decisions or confirmation of those decisions.
- Employers should act consistently.
- Employers should carry out any necessary investigations to establish the facts of the case.

- Employers should inform employees of the basis of the problem and give them an opportunity to put their case in response before any decisions are made.
- Employers should allow employees to be accompanied at any formal disciplinary or grievance meeting.
- Employers should allow an employee to appeal against any formal decision made.

It is useful to set out any specific expectations of a senior executive and the implications if those expectations are not met in the contract of employment. In *Dunn & Anor v AAH Limited [2010] EWCA Civ 183*, the executives' contract of employment specifically stated that they could be dismissed for gross misconduct if they were 'guilty of dishonesty or incompetence or wilful neglect of duty'. The Managing Director and Finance Director became aware of a possible fraud against the organisation and did not follow the risk management guidelines and report it to the parent company. They were dismissed for gross misconduct. The Court of Appeal concluded that the dismissals were fair. By not reporting the potential fraud, the executives had breached the implied term of mutual trust and confidence, which is at the heart of every contract of employment.

Make sure that you are specific in your expectations of senior executives, and spell out anything that could mean that they are in breach of contract.

Summary dismissal

Where an allegation of gross misconduct is established following a disciplinary process, the outcome is usually immediate (summary) dismissal. This means that no notice pay is payable to the senior executive in these circumstances. Whilst it will only be on rare occasions that a gross misconduct allegation against a senior executive makes it all the way to an open dismissal, it can be very important to settlement discussions to communicate that the open option on the table would involve immediate termination with no payment of notice pay.

Chapter 10
An exploration of fair dismissal: redundancy

Redundancy is one of the potentially fair reasons for dismissal under the *Employment Rights Act 1996*. An employee is dismissed by reason of redundancy if they are dismissed for one of the following reasons:

- The employer has stopped, or plans to stop, running the business for the purposes for which the employee is employed (business closure).
- The employer has stopped, or plans to stop, running the business at the place the employee works (location closure).
- The employer no longer needs (or expects to no longer need) as many employees to do that type of work or to do it at the place where the employee is employed.

It is likely that senior executives are going to be more expensive to employ than other employees. If it is not possible to meet that ongoing cost, then there could be a redundancy situation.

In *TNS UK Ltd v Swainston UKEAT/0603/12/BA*, the employee worked as a Business Development Director. It was decided not to continue providing the services that she was responsible for, and therefore, she was dismissed due to redundancy. She was in a pool of one, so there was no selection process. The Employment Appeal Tribunal found that this was a redundancy situation. The reasons behind many redundancies are financial.

The employer must follow a fair process by consulting with the executive regarding the redundancy and carrying out a fair selection process. If redundancy is the impetus behind the suggestion that a senior executive should exit the business, then you should first consider the appropriate pool: is the executive in a stand-alone role, or do they need to be pooled for selection?

Bumping should also be considered. 'Bumping', in a redundancy context, is when an executive whose job is redundant is moved into another role in the organisation, bumping the incumbent of that job out of their role and therefore meaning that individual is dismissed due to redundancy.

When managing redundancies with senior executives, this could mean that a senior executive is kept in the organisation, but a more junior employee loses their job because the senior executive is moved into the more junior role.

Payments due on redundancy

A senior executive who is made redundant is entitled to receive full notice pay in line with their contract of employment. They are also likely to be classified as a 'good leaver' under any shareholder's agreement or LTIP arrangement – although this should always be checked.

A redundant executive who has at least two years' continuous service at the termination date is entitled to a statutory redundancy payment, calculated by reference to weekly pay, age and length of service. Weekly pay is capped for these purposes, currently (April 2025) at £719 per week.

In practice, the amount of a statutory redundancy award will not be a significant proportion of a severance payment to a senior executive. But there may also be an entitlement to a contractual redundancy payment. This may be calculated based on the statutory redundancy payment but without the limit on a week's pay, or by using some other formula. The existence of any such scheme should always be checked at an early stage.

Chapter 11

An exploration of fair dismissal: capability

Capability is another potentially fair reason for dismissal under the *Employment Rights Act 1996*. Capability dismissals are relatively rare at senior executive level. Underperformance at this level can be difficult to confront and manage formally. Senior executives enjoy a high degree of autonomy, with performance that is less easy to measure or benchmark objectively. Their seniority can also make managing performance issues uncomfortable, particularly where the individual is well-regarded personally or has been in post for some time.

Where capability concerns arise, they are usually a slow burn. A fair dismissal for poor performance will almost always require a formal performance improvement plan (PIP), clear targets, appropriate support and a sustained period of monitoring. This can take months to execute properly and requires real commitment from senior leadership. It also means tolerating poor performance for a significant period, which, at this level, can be commercially damaging. A poorly performing executive can affect strategy, morale, financial results and reputation.

For these reasons, capability concerns are sometimes used as the starting point for a protected conversation (see Chapter 13) rather than being pursued as a formal process.

Where the business has lost confidence in a senior executive's performance, a managed exit is frequently seen as the cleaner and safer option, especially where the risks of protracted performance management outweigh the benefits of a formal route to dismissal.

That said, if the business does decide to pursue an open capability dismissal, it must ensure that the process is fair and well documented. This includes identifying specific concerns, communicating them clearly, offering a realistic opportunity to improve and evidencing both support and monitoring over time. The *Acas Code of Practice* on disciplinary and grievance procedures applies to capability dismissals and should be followed.

Chapter 12
Common procedural issues with senior executive dismissals

Dismissing a senior executive can be tricky, not only because of the legal and business angles but also when it comes to process. It's easy to see internal procedures as a box-ticking exercise, especially if there's already been a conversation about the person leaving. But it's important to get the process right. Senior staff are entitled to fair treatment, just like anyone else, and if things go wrong here, it can increase the risk of legal claims and throw off an agreed exit.

Here are some key procedural issues that may need to be considered.

1. Legal representation at disciplinary hearings

Generally, employees are entitled to be accompanied at disciplinary hearings by a work colleague or trade union representative under section 10 of the *Employment Relations Act 1999*. There is no automatic right to legal representation, even for senior executives.

That said, certain situations, particularly where a dismissal may have career-ending consequences, may justify a broader right to legal representation under Article 6 of the *European Convention on Human Rights* (the right to a fair hearing).

Key case law includes:

- *R (G) v Governors of X School [2011] UKSC 30* – The Supreme Court held that Article 6 could apply to internal disciplinary processes where the outcome may effectively bar an individual from their profession (here, teaching).
- *Mattu v University Hospitals of Coventry and Warwickshire NHS Trust [2012] EWCA Civ 641* – Here, the Court of Appeal found that Article 6 did not apply because the disciplinary outcome did not determine the individual's right to practise medicine; the GMC retained ultimate control.
- *Kulkarni v Milton Keynes Hospital NHS Foundation Trust [2009] EWCA Civ 789* – The Court recognised that NHS doctors had a contractual disciplinary procedure that permitted legal representation, reinforcing the importance of checking sector-specific rules.

If the outcome of a disciplinary process could end a professional career or bar the individual from their industry (particularly in regulated sectors), there is a chance that refusing legal representation might breach their Article 6 rights, so you may need to justify any refusal carefully.

2. Authority to dismiss

For a dismissal to be legally valid, you must make sure that the person making the decision has actual authority to do so.

This is especially important when the employee in question operates at executive or board level.

Check:

- The contract of employment or service agreement
- The company's Articles of Association
- Any relevant delegation of authority or board resolutions

In listed or regulated companies, dismissals may need Board approval, or, in rare cases, shareholder involvement. Where HR professionals or legal teams act without clarity on authority, the company risks a claim for breach of contract, or reputational damage if the dismissal is later found to be unauthorised.

3. Separation of roles in the process

Where a formal disciplinary process is followed, best practice is to have different individuals managing each stage:

- One person to investigate
- One to chair the disciplinary hearing
- Another to hear the appeal

This becomes particularly challenging when the individual under scrutiny is part of the senior leadership team and most potential decision-makers are their peers or direct reports. In some cases, businesses may need to bring in an external investigator or chair, or consider a non-executive director or board member to maintain impartiality. The HR Inner Circle maintains a list of independent investigators, which you can find at https://go.danielbarnett.com/investigators.

Conclusion

Procedural fairness matters just as much, if not more, when the person under scrutiny sits at the top of the organisational chart. Failing to take the time to get the basics right (authority, impartiality, representation) can result in legal exposure. Even when a negotiated exit seems inevitable, a fair and transparent process ensures the business is protected – and sets the right tone.

Chapter 13

Doing a deal: protected conversations and without prejudice

Senior executive exits are rarely handled through an open process. Commercial pressures usually prompt businesses to focus quickly on 'doing a deal'. However, there are clear legal rules that govern how employers should manage this. When handled properly, an 'off the record' approach can save time and money, allowing both sides to part on good terms. But what are the ground rules? How can employers hold these difficult conversations with senior executives in a way that is effective and legally safe?

Without prejudice

Employers can rely on the 'without prejudice' rule to protect communications about settlement from disclosure if the following elements exist:

1. There is a dispute
2. An offer is made
3. The offer is a genuine attempt to settle the dispute

If an employer initiates a conversation to exit a senior executive, and it's the first time the issue is being raised, it's hard to argue that this is a genuine attempt to settle an existing dispute – because there *is* no dispute at that point. While a dispute may arise by the end of the conversation, it doesn't exist at the start, meaning the opening part of the discussion can't be considered 'off the record' or protected by the 'without prejudice' rule.

For a 'dispute' to arise, there needs to be a difference of opinion and a lack of agreement. In *BNP Paribas v Mezzotero [2004] IRLR 508*, it was held that the act of raising a grievance, on its own, does not mean that there is a dispute between the employee and the employer in a 'without prejudice' sense. A grievance is the raising of a concern. It is not a 'dispute' in and of itself, although it may become one if the employee disagrees with the employer's response. There is usually a tipping point in these situations. (For what it's worth, this seems a silly rule. Obviously, a formal grievance should be enough to establish a 'dispute'. But the law does not agree.)

If you intend for a meeting to be 'without prejudice', you should say this at the outset. If a meeting starts without dispute, but a dispute develops, then you should be ready to pause and confirm that the rest of the meeting will be without prejudice.

Pre-termination negotiations

Where there is no existing dispute, the 'without prejudice' rule does not apply, so any conversation about settling with the executive would be at risk of being disclosed. Even worse, just approaching the executive could give rise to a claim; if the executive is upset by it, they could potentially resign and claim constructive dismissal.

This is where the idea of 'pre-termination negotiations' comes in. Under section 111A of the *Employment Rights Act 1996*, you can hold a 'pre-termination negotiation' with an executive and make a settlement offer to them *before* any dispute arises. The facts and details of the conversation can't be used in later ordinary unfair dismissal proceedings, unless the employer has acted improperly.

'Pre-termination negotiations' are a poor substitute for 'without prejudice'. They only protect discussions from disclosure as part of ordinary unfair dismissal claims. If the executive alleges some form of discrimination (or any other type of employment claim), then the fact and content of the discussion are disclosable. But they can be a useful tool to get the ball rolling before a 'dispute' has arisen. It is likely, by the time you get to the end of a pre-termination negotiation meeting, that you will be in dispute anyway, and the 'without prejudice' rule will have kicked in. It's always a good idea to reference both terms ('without prejudice' and 'pre-termination negotiations') in all discussions and correspondence flowing from an initial meeting.

A handy comparison table

	Without prejudice	**Protected conversation**
Source of principle	Common law	Statute: Section 111A of the *Employment Rights Act 1996*
Dispute required?	Yes	No
Fact of conversation protected from disclosure?	Probably not	Yes
Content of conversation protected from disclosure?	Yes	Yes
Claims covered	Prevents disclosure in all employment tribunal claims	Prevents disclosure in ordinary unfair dismissal claims only
Restrictions on protection	No protection if there has been unambiguous impropriety	No protection if there has been improper behaviour

Limits to protection: 'Improper behaviour' and 'unambiguous impropriety'

If the 'without prejudice' rule applies, then usually the content of settlement discussions between the parties cannot be used in later legal proceedings. But there are limits. An employer cannot rely on this protection if there has been any unambiguous impropriety. That generally means illegal behaviour or serious misuse of power. It's a narrow exception. In 2021, the Court of Appeal said this exception only applies in "truly exceptional" cases (*Motorola v Hytera Communications [2021] EWCA Civ 11*).

In *Swiss Re Corporate Solutions v Sommer [2022] EAT 78*, an employment tribunal found that an employer had acted improperly when, during settlement talks, its solicitors sent a letter to Mrs Sommer with exaggerated allegations of serious misconduct, suggesting possible criminal or regulatory action. The tribunal ruled that this behaviour meant the employer lost the benefit of without prejudice protection.

The employer appealed. The Employment Appeal Tribunal disagreed with the tribunal and said that although the allegations were exaggerated, they weren't completely baseless. That meant the employer had not crossed the line into unambiguous impropriety, and the without prejudice rule still applied.

The protection afforded to pre-termination negotiations under section 111A of the *Employment Rights Act 1996* is also limited. Employers cannot rely on it if there has been any 'improper behaviour'. The *Acas Code of Practice* on settlement agreements provides useful guidance on improper behaviour. The concept is wider than 'unambiguous impropriety'. Examples of improper behaviour suggested by Acas include:

- All forms of harassment, bullying and intimidation, including using offensive words or aggressive behaviour.

- Physical assault or the threat of physical assault and other criminal behaviour.
- All forms of victimisation.
- Discrimination because of age, sex, race, disability, sexual orientation, religion or belief, transgender, pregnancy and maternity and marriage or civil partnership.
- Putting undue pressure on a party. For instance, not giving the reasonable time for consideration (suggested to be at least 10 working days in the *Acas Code of Practice*), or an employer saying before any form of disciplinary process has begun that if a settlement proposal is rejected, then the employee will be dismissed.

In *Gallagher v McKinnon Auto and Tyres [2024] EAT 174*, the Employment Appeal Tribunal looked at 'improper behaviour' in the context of pre-termination negotiations. The claimant was a Branch Manager who had been off sick. When he returned to work, the employer said his role was no longer needed and proposed a redundancy process. At an 'off-the-record' meeting, the claimant was offered a settlement agreement and given 48 hours to decide, with an indication that redundancy would follow if he refused. The claimant declined the offer and was later dismissed for redundancy. He brought a claim for unfair dismissal and tried to rely on the settlement discussions as part of his case.

The tribunal said the discussions were protected pre-termination negotiations and couldn't be used as evidence because there had been no improper behaviour.

The claimant appealed, arguing there was improper behaviour because he was told the meeting was a 'return to work' meeting and was caught off guard, he was only given 48 hours to decide, and he was told he'd be made redundant if he didn't accept the offer.

The Employment Appeal Tribunal rejected the appeal. It said that points 1 and 2 did not amount to improper behaviour in this case. On point 3, the Tribunal emphasised the need to distinguish redundancy from disciplinary cases. The *Acas Code of Practice* says it may be improper to tell an employee they'll be dismissed if they reject an offer – but that refers to disciplinary situations. Here, the employer had said the role was redundant, but that didn't mean dismissal was certain. There was still a possibility of alternative employment.

Checklist

Whenever you are thinking about holding either a without-prejudice meeting or pre-termination negotiation with an executive, use this checklist as a useful starting point:

- Is 'without prejudice' engaged? Is there a 'dispute' already? Make sure that you label your meeting correctly.
- Review the background to the situation arising. Does it disclose any risk over and above unfair dismissal (for example, discrimination or whistleblowing)?
- Write a clear script to use in a first meeting to explain why a settlement is being proposed. The script should avoid making it sound like a final decision has already been made. Instead, it should leave room to start a formal process if the executive doesn't accept the offer.

- What are the facts and figures? Pull together a table setting out the executive's contractual entitlements in terms of notice pay and accrued holiday pay. Also consider their statutory redundancy entitlement, as this figure mirrors the basic award an executive would generally receive if they successfully claimed unfair dismissal.
- Consider which elements can be paid tax free and which elements will need to go through payroll. Tax-free payments are limited to £30,000 under settlement agreements.
- Consider any wider implications given that the individual is a senior executive. Are they a statutory director? Are there any provisions in the business's remuneration policy or elsewhere that might limit what can be offered? How will you go about removing them as a director? Are they a shareholder? What does any shareholder's agreement say about exit as an employee?
- Agree your top line so that any negotiation is conducted between known internal parameters.
- Make sure that written and traceable internal correspondence is kept to a minimum.
- Make sure that all documentation sent to the executive is labelled 'without prejudice'
- Consider lining up a solicitor to prepare a settlement agreement so that you can move quickly if the executive is interested in settling.

Chapter 14

Doing a deal: how to start a negotiation and what to offer

When negotiating a senior executive exit, it is important to keep track of exactly what is on the table at any given time (i.e. what has been offered and what has been rejected). If you don't do this, then you risk a situation where the executive thinks you have reached settlement A and you think you have reached settlement B, you draw up the paperwork and then realise you have agreed something different to each other. This can waste valuable time and cause negotiations to lose momentum.

How do you stop this? Here are some tips:

- Always set out any offer in writing. Even if the offer is initially made verbally, you should follow it up with written confirmation. It is harder for people to get confused if something is written down.
- Make sure that any offers made (whether verbal or written) are stated to be 'without prejudice and subject to contract'. Offers generally deal with headline terms only – basically, the money side of things – but you want to make sure that the executive knows that there will be 'window dressing' around the monetary offer and they will be required to sign a full settlement agreement.

- Understand how offers and counter-offers work. If you receive an offer from an executive and wish to 'counter', once you make your counter-offer, the executive's original offer is rejected and is no longer on the table. If the executive rejects your counter-offer, you cannot then go back and say, "Ok then, we'll accept your original offer." You would technically need to make that offer yourself, and the executive would be entitled to reject it.

Another aspect of the mechanics of negotiation is how long you leave an offer open for. Should you impose a deadline for acceptance? Negotiations can't drag on forever. The *Acas Code of Practice* on settlement agreements suggests a period of ten calendar days for the employee to consider the settlement agreement and receive independent advice – although this isn't mandatory and a shorter period might be necessary depending on the surrounding circumstances.

Managing expectations

How much should you offer as a starting point? A full risk assessment gives you the parameters within which the business is comfortable to negotiate. This does not mean that you should go in with your best offer straight away – this leaves you nowhere to go in negotiation if your position is rejected. Likewise, you don't want to pitch an opening offer too low, as this could be insulting to the executive and escalate tension and conflict.

The reality is that there is a balance to be struck between controlling expectations and insulting the executive's sense of worth.

The question of an appropriate opening offer is, by its very nature, case-specific. However, here are a few pointers to help you get to your opening figure:

- A common approach is to start at a sum between 50% and 70% of the maximum you would be prepared or can afford to pay, so you have some wriggle room when negotiating.
- You know the executive. What baggage are they bringing to the table? For example, are they bad with money? Will a quick resolution with prompt payment be attractive to them? If so, consider going in hard and fast with an attractive financial sum that is only available for acceptance for a short period. Are they more worried about getting another job than the money? If that is the case, you may want to focus on the 'softer' elements of your offer – for example, a reference or outplacement services – and perhaps hold back slightly on any financial offer.
- Stress any elements of the offer that show you have considered the executive and their unique position, for example, an offer to structure the payment for tax efficiency or to agree a waiver of post-termination restrictions. This shows empathy and can help negotiations go smoothly.

Setting the tone

If you are negotiating with the executive or their representative, you need to be clear, confident and assertive about your position. There are different ways to approach a settlement agreement. When the employee is in a senior role, a firm but respectful tone often works best, whether you are speaking to them directly or dealing with their adviser. Presenting the process as a joint effort to reach a mutually acceptable outcome can help things run more smoothly.

As with any negotiation, you need to be clear about what you want to achieve and how far you are willing to go to get there. This involves weighing the risks and costs of not reaching an agreement against the benefits of doing so.

Once you have worked this out, you will be in a stronger position. You will know your goals, the key risks and your non-negotiables.

If the executive is still employed during the talks, it is important to keep any open processes going. This might include disciplinary, consultation or performance management procedures. Do not let these go quiet while you negotiate. Keeping them active often helps keep the executive engaged. It also sends a clear signal that the business is prepared to continue with formal steps if needed and is not relying only on a negotiated exit.

Negotiation is a bit like a dance. Both sides are testing each other and working out how far the other can be pushed. The more prepared and focused you are, the more likely you are to achieve a deal that works for your organisation.

Chapter 15
Doing a deal: settlement agreements

Settlement agreements are legally binding contracts used to end the employment relationship (or settle disputes) on agreed terms. Their main feature is that they waive an individual's right to make a claim to a court or employment tribunal on the matters covered in the agreement.

For a settlement agreement to be legally valid (and prevent an executive from being able to bring tribunal proceedings), it must meet the following conditions:

- The agreement must be in writing.
- The agreement must relate to a particular complaint or proceedings. (Note: Simply saying that the agreement is in 'full and final settlement of all claims' will not be good enough to contract out of employment tribunal claims. A settlement agreement has to specifically state the claims that it covers – although it is recommended to include a general waiver as well.)
- The employee must have received advice from a relevant independent adviser (this is usually a qualified lawyer, but it can be certain certified trade union officials or a certified and authorised advice centre worker).

- The independent adviser must have a current contract of insurance or professional indemnity insurance in place.
- The agreement must identify the adviser.
- The agreement must state that it satisfies the statutory conditions regulating settlement agreements.

Settlement agreements are generally drafted by solicitors, although Acas has a template available on its website: https://www.acas.org.uk/settlement-agreement-template.

At what point in negotiations should you produce a settlement agreement?

If you are working to a specific deadline, for example, if the executive's exit needs to be completed by a certain date, it is best to put the written settlement agreement on the table early. This sets out clearly what you want from the process and what you are offering. While letters outlining proposed terms can help start the conversation, they have their limits. The executive will need legal advice, and that advice will be based on the actual agreement. So the earlier you share it, the better.

If you do send a draft settlement agreement, make sure it is clearly marked 'without prejudice and subject to formal agreement'. This protects the confidentiality of the negotiation. The draft agreement should also include a clause confirming that it only becomes legally binding once it has been signed by both parties and the executive's legal adviser.

What can you get out of this? Making the settlement agreement work for you

Settlement agreements are not just about what you offer the executive. You should also think about what terms you want to include to protect the business. Below are examples of clauses you may want to include. Suggested wording for some of them can be found in Appendix 3.

- **Non-disparagement clause** – You may want to stop the executive from speaking badly about the business after they leave. These clauses are hard to enforce, but they act as a useful deterrent.
- **Post-termination restrictions and confidentiality** – This is your chance to restate or strengthen existing clauses from the contract, or to introduce new ones. If the contract is weak in these areas or contains no restrictions, now is the time to fix that. You will need to offer a payment to support any new restrictions. This payment is taxable, so make sure you set aside part of the total settlement amount to cover it.
- **Return of company property** – The agreement should confirm that the executive has returned all items belonging to the business. A clean break means nothing left behind.
- **Job-seeking status** – If you made your offer assuming the executive was not yet in new employment, you may want them to confirm that this is true. If they have already secured a job, that may have affected your offer.

- **Set-off clause** – If the settlement includes a sum for lost earnings, you might want to include a clause allowing you to set off part of the payment if the executive finds a new job within a certain timeframe.
- **Past conduct warranty** – You may want the executive to confirm they have not already done something that would have changed your approach to negotiations, or justified dismissal had you known about it.
- **Tax indemnity** – This is a standard clause. You will be paying a sum on the understanding that it is tax-free under current rules. If that turns out to be wrong, you will want the executive to cover any extra tax due.
- **Entire agreement clause** – This clause confirms that the settlement agreement is the full and final agreement between the parties. It prevents the executive from referring to earlier offers or emails and trying to claim more than what is in the final document.
- **Director resignation clause** – If the executive is a company director, you will want their resignation in writing. These resignation letters are often included as schedules in the settlement agreement.
- **Shareholder arrangements** – If the executive is also a shareholder, you may need a separate agreement to deal with their shares. The settlement agreement might include a simple clause confirming that the executive will be treated as a 'good leaver' under any existing shareholder agreement.

Chapter 16

Special situations and how to deal with them

When dismissing a senior executive, some situations require additional care. This chapter explores several issues that arise frequently and provides practical guidance on how to navigate them.

1. Resignation as a director / removal as a shareholder

As covered in Chapter 3, the termination of a senior executive's employment relationship with a business does not automatically end any statutory directorships they might hold. You will want to secure a letter of resignation from the executive, resigning from any directorships.

If you can have any input into the form of the letter of resignation, you should seek to include a 'waiver of claims', where the director releases all and any claims or rights of action of any nature against the company arising out of the termination of their office. If the letter does include a waiver, it should be signed as a deed, which will protect the company if there are any disputes about consideration provided for such a waiver. A draft letter can be found in Appendix 4. If you are entering into a settlement agreement, make the signature of appropriately worded resignation letters a condition of the agreement.

Where the resigning director is also an officer of any subsidiaries, it is best practice for separate letters of resignation to be used for each.

If the director is also a shareholder of the company and is required to transfer their shares in the company because of their resignation, the company's register of members, and possibly its register of persons with significant control (if relevant), will need to be updated following that transfer and any relevant Companies House filings made.

2. Early retirement benefits in final salary pension schemes

Senior executives with access to final salary (defined benefit) pension schemes may have enhanced early retirement benefits, often triggered by dismissal, redundancy or a negotiated retirement. Where an early retirement pension is more valuable than a severance payment, this can significantly affect the structure of any settlement.

Employers should:

- Understand the scheme rules – including eligibility criteria for early retirement.
- Liaise with pension scheme administrators early to obtain projections.
- Consider the overall value of early retirement against any proposed termination package.

- Ensure any offer is clearly documented and reviewed for tax implications.

Avoid making representations about pension benefits without first confirming the legal position – final salary pensions are fiendishly complicated. Expert advice is often needed from the scheme trustees or administrators.

3. Retirement: tax implications on settlement sums

When a senior executive's exit is described as a retirement, this can affect how any payments are taxed. HMRC may look closely at large settlement payments to decide whether they are earnings (which are fully taxable) or termination payments (which may qualify for the £30,000 tax exemption under the *Income Tax (Earnings and Pensions) Act 2003* (ITEPA)).

Any lump sum, including an ex gratia payment, paid to someone who retires or is close to retirement, could be taxed in full under sections 393 and 394 of ITEPA. These sections state that any "relevant benefits" received in connection with retirement are treated as employment income. This includes sums paid on, after or in anticipation of retirement, and the rules apply where the payment is made through any employer-financed retirement benefits scheme. The word "scheme" is interpreted broadly. In *Forsyth v HMRC [2021] UKUT 0104*, the First-tier Tribunal held that a compromise agreement could count as a scheme for this purpose.

This means that making an ex gratia payment tax free may be difficult in retirement cases. There are limited exceptions, such as payments made for ill health or disability during employment, but these will not always apply.

Employers should:

- Be clear on whether the exit is being treated as a retirement or a termination.
- Take tax advice on how to structure payments (for example, bonus deferral or share vesting).
- Avoid using language in the agreement that confuses retirement with dismissal.

4. Provision of references in regulated roles

In regulated sectors (all firms regulated by the FCA or the PRA), reference obligations are governed by formal regulatory rules. Under the FCA/PRA Senior Managers & Certification Regime, employers must provide detailed regulatory references covering six years of employment history. A business has an obligation to provide a regulatory reference as soon as reasonably practicable if it receives a request from another firm that is considering appointing someone to a controlled function, certifying them as fit and proper or appointing them to certain other positions, including board director.

Points to note:

- The reference must disclose relevant disciplinary findings, even post-departure.
- There is no duty to provide a standard 'neutral' reference if the role is regulated.

- A negotiated reference cannot override regulatory obligations – be careful not to promise more than you can lawfully deliver.

5. Share plans and long-term incentive plans (LTIPs)

Share plans and LTIPs are delayed compensation strategies that a business may use to motivate employees over an extended period. They can form a substantial part of many senior executives' reward packages. When a senior executive is dismissed, the impact that the dismissal has on these benefits needs to be clearly analysed.

Most employee share plans and stand-alone employee share award contracts state that share awards or share options will be lost on the termination of employment (or on giving or receiving notice). However, an executive will usually be allowed to keep share awards on ceasing employment in certain circumstances, such as:

- Being made redundant
- Leaving the company because of illness or disability

These are usually known as 'good leaver' circumstances. In addition, the company operating the share plan (usually the employer or the employer's parent company) often has discretion under the plan rules to allow an award, or part of an award, to be retained by the executive after termination of employment.

It is worth checking whether the share plan provisions or the contract of employment contain a *Micklefield* clause.

This is a clause excluding the business's liability for loss of an executive's rights under an employee share plan or share award contract caused by any termination of (or notice to terminate) employment. This was held to be enforceable in *Micklefield v SAC Technology [1990] 1 WLR 1002*. But it doesn't provide complete protection. If the employer has discretion under the plan as to how to treat the executive's option/award on exit, then the executive is still able to claim for damages caused by the way in which a business exercised (or refused to exercise) its discretion to permit the exercise of a share option, or the vesting or retention of shares under a share award, after termination of employment.

Employers should:

- Review plan rules early – many tie eligibility to 'good leaver' status.
- Be aware of timing issues around performance periods and vesting dates.
- Document any discretionary decisions clearly, particularly around retention or forfeiture.

Dismissal for misconduct may trigger bad leaver provisions; in other cases, it might be negotiable as part of a settlement.

Chapter 17

Putting your best foot forward: top tips for getting it right from the start

The best way to avoid a difficult exit is to make good decisions at the start of the relationship.

This chapter sets out our tips for recruiting well, using probationary periods effectively and getting the contract right.

1. Pre-employment checks

Always carry out appropriate pre-employment checks for the role. For example, DBS checks may be needed for roles involving vulnerable people. References can also be useful – even if vague, they may highlight concerns to follow up. A reference doesn't need to be glowing, but it must be true, accurate and fair. Take note of what's not said, and feel free to follow up if something seems off. If a reference is not 'glowing', is this the referee telling you, indirectly, that there is a problem?

2. Probationary periods

Include a probationary period in the contract. This gives you time to assess fit and performance. Typically, this should be at least six months. Be clear on what success looks like and reserve the right to extend the probation if needed. Make it clear that failure to pass probation may lead to dismissal without a full disciplinary process. Courts recognise that employers aren't expected to provide extensive support during probation, but they should act reasonably and give clear feedback.

Be aware that should unfair dismissal become a 'day 1' employment right, as proposed in the Employment Rights Bill, the special status of probationary periods is likely to change. Employees will have the right not to be unfairly dismissed from the very first day of employment. There will be no way of bypassing due process when the employment relationship is in its early days. At the time of publication, much remains to be fleshed out regarding this proposed change in the law. There may be a residual role for the probationary period in some form, as the Bill includes provision for an 'initial period of employment' which is likely to cover the first nine months. During the initial period of employment, a 'light touch' dismissal process may be sufficient to avoid an unfair dismissal. With the idea of the initial period of employment floating around, it looks like, even if the law changes, there will still be scope to evaluate conduct and performance more critically in the early stages of the employment relationship.

3. The contract

Before employment starts, ensure the contract includes:

- **Notice** – Set sensible notice periods and include the right to use PILON or garden leave.

- **Confidentiality** – Protect sensitive business information.
- **Restrictive covenants** – Limit what the executive can do after leaving.
- **Gross misconduct** – Define key examples relevant to your organisation.

Getting these basics right makes managing any later difficulties much easier.

Appendix 1

Dismissing senior executives: a checklist

	Item to review	Supporting documents needed	Implications / HR comments	HR comments (for completion)
Corporate status	Is the individual a statutory director under the *Companies Act 2006*?	Articles of Association, Companies House records	Need to check procedure for removal/resignation as a director. May require board resolution to remove and Companies House update.	
	Is the individual a statutory director of any other companies in the Group?	Articles of Association, Companies House records	Need to check procedure for removal/resignation as a director. May require board resolution to remove and Companies House update.	

	Item to review	Supporting documents needed	Implications / HR comments	HR comments (for completion)
Corporate status	Is there a provision in the employment contract allowing the business to act as the director's attorney to effect any resignation as a director?	Service agreement	The existence of this clause can allow the business to control the exiting executive's removal as a director.	
	Does the individual have a Directors' Loan Account?	Articles of Association, any Directors' Loan Account	Exit will need to include consideration of repaying or writing off any loan. Tax implications need to be considered.	
	Is the individual also a shareholder?	Shareholders' agreement, share register	May require share buyback or transfer agreement; tax planning implications	
	Is the business regulated, and does the individual hold a regulated position?	PRA and FCA registration records	There are strict rules on references where a person has held a regulated position in a regulated business.	

	Item to review	Supporting documents needed	Implications / HR comments	HR comments (for completion)
Contractual terms	Does the individual have a contract of employment / service agreement?	Copy of signed agreement	Sets out rights on termination, entitlements and obligations.	
	Are there restrictive covenants in place?	Contract / service agreement, side agreements	Important for post-exit protections – consider enforceability.	
	Is there a PILON (payment in lieu of notice) clause?	Contract of employment	Enables clean termination with an agreed sum; tax treatment must be checked.	
	Is there a garden leave clause?	Contract of employment	Allows removal of access and sensitive information during notice period.	
	What is the notice period (contractual/statutory)?	Contract, employee record	Affects timing and cost of exit.	

	Item to review	Supporting documents needed	Implications / HR comments	HR comments (for completion)
Remunera-tion	Is the individual eligible for a bonus?	Bonus plan rules, past bonus letters	Check entitlement, whether discretionary, and how maternity/sickness/leave affects it.	
	Is the individual on a commission scheme?	Commission rules, past earnings	May require pro-rated payout or be withheld – check justification.	
	Is the individual part of an LTIP or incentive scheme?	Scheme rules, award letters, vesting schedule	Check good/bad leaver terms and market disclosure requirements (if listed company).	

	Item to review	Supporting documents needed	Implications / HR comments	HR comments (for completion)
Employment rights and claims	Does the individual have two or more years' service with the business?	Employee records, service agreement	Currently only employees with two or more years of service have ordinary unfair dismissal rights. The risk of claims is reduced if they are not eligible, and this can impact negotiations.	
	What would the individual's basic award be?	Length of service details, ready reckoner	The basic award for unfair dismissal mirrors statutory redundancy entitlement. Getting an idea of the amount payable can help to frame negotiations.	
	Does the business have a 'potentially fair reason' to rely upon when seeking to dismiss?	Employment Rights Act 1996.	There are five potentially fair reasons for dismissal in law: conduct, capability, redundancy, illegality and some other substantial reason. HR needs to consider which of these is in play when opening negotiations.	

	Item to review	Supporting documents needed	Implications / HR comments	HR comments (for completion)
Employment rights and claims	Is the individual a disabled person?	HR records, employee disclosure	Disabled employees have additional legal protections under the *Equality Act 2010*. If the business is considering following an open dismissal process, the impact of any disability and the risk that the behaviour at issue might arise from it need to be considered. Medical advice may need to be taken.	

	Item to review	Supporting documents needed	Implications / HR comments	HR comments (for completion)
Employment rights and claims	Is there any other disclosed discrimination or whistleblowing risk?	HR records	Employees are protected from discrimination covering nine different characteristics. Alongside disability (see above), these comprise sex, race, religion or belief, sexual orientation, gender reassignment, age, marriage and civil partnership, pregnancy and maternity. Additionally, employees are entitled to be protected from detriment or dismissal by reason of having blown the whistle about potential wrongdoing within the business. If the executive might have made a protected disclosure, then HR needs to be comfortable that any proposed exit is in no way linked to it.	

	Item to review	Supporting documents needed	Implications / HR comments	HR comments (for completion)
Settlement	Is there a dispute?	n/a	The without prejudice principle (allowing off-the-record discussion around settlement at low risk) is only engaged where the parties are in dispute. Where there is no dispute, the employer must fall back on the much narrower protected conversation rules under section 111A of the *Employment Rights Act 1996*.	
	Is there a possibility that the exit might be considered a retirement?	Age of employee. Future plans.	This can impact the tax treatment of any termination payment offered and needs to be considered at an early stage.	

Appendix 2

Useful template service agreement clauses

Important note – please read

The template clauses in this appendix are provided for general guidance only. Every situation is different, and what works for one employer or executive may not be appropriate for another.

Before using or adapting any of these clauses, you should take your own independent legal advice. Employment law and tax law can be complex, and the wording of contractual clauses may have legal or financial consequences that are not immediately obvious. You are responsible for ensuring that any clauses you use are properly drafted and tailored to your specific context.

1. Intellectual property

1.1. When carrying out your role (whether during your core working hours or not), you may, by yourself or with someone else, design, write or otherwise create works that generate intellectual property rights. These rights include copyright, patents, trademarks and design rights.

1.2. You shall give us full written details of such works and any and all works which may give rise to intellectual property rights made wholly or partially by you at any time during the course of your employment with us.

1.3. You agree that we will own any intellectual property in the work you do in the course of your employment. If, for any reason, any such intellectual property doesn't automatically belong to us, you agree that you hold it on trust for us and will do all acts and sign all documents as might be necessary to transfer the intellectual property to us.

1.4. You agree to waive any moral rights in the work you have carried out, or will carry out, for us.

1.5. You irrevocably appoint us to be your attorney in your name and on your behalf to execute documents, use your name and do all things which are necessary or desirable for us to obtain for ourselves or our nominee the full benefit of this clause.[1]

2. Payment in lieu of notice

2.1. Instead of requiring you to work your notice, we may decide to pay you in lieu of notice, bringing your employment to an end there and then.

2.2. Your payment in lieu of notice will be made up of your net basic salary for the notice period. It will not

[1] If you include a power of attorney clause in the contract, then the contract must be executed as a deed in order for the clause to have effect.

include payments such as [[bonuses], [commission] and [payments representing benefits [(such as [insert relevant payments])]] that would be due during the notice period, or any holiday pay for days that would have accrued during the notice period.

2.3. We may decide to pay you in lieu of notice in instalments. If you start a new job at any point before the final instalment is paid (and you must make every reasonable effort to find another source of income), you must tell us straight away. We will reduce the amount we pay you accordingly.

2.4. If we discover that we had grounds for ending your employment without notice, we may withhold any payment in lieu (whether a single payment or instalments) and may require you to pay back any element of payment in lieu that you have already received from us.

3. Resignation of directorships on termination

3.1. On termination of your employment (however arising) or earlier on request, you shall resign immediately without compensation from any office in [the Company OR any Group Company].

3.2. You hereby irrevocably appoint us to be your attorney to execute and do any such instrument or thing and generally to use your name for the purpose of giving us or our nominee the full benefit of this clause.[2]

[2] If you include a power of attorney clause in the contract, then the contract must

4. Effect of termination on deferred benefits

4.1. On termination of your employment (however arising), you shall not be entitled to any compensation for the loss of any rights or benefits under any [share option, bonus, long-term incentive plan or other] profit sharing scheme operated by [the Company OR any Group Company] in which you may participate.[3]

5. Garden leave

5.1. We may decide to put you on Garden Leave for some or all of your notice period.

5.2. Garden Leave means that you should not come to work, but you remain employed and entitled to your contractual benefits and subject to your contractual obligations (apart from the requirement to carry out work).

5.3. During any period of Garden Leave, unless you are informed in writing otherwise:

5.3.1. We shall be under no obligation to provide any work to you.

5.3.2. We may require you to carry out alternative duties.

---

be executed as a deed in order for the clause to have effect

[3] This clause attempts to exclude an employee's contractual right to claim for loss of benefits under share option, profit sharing or bonus schemes that flow from the termination of their employment. Such clauses have been enforced. However, they don't stop an employee from claiming these losses as part of a claim for compensation for unfair dismissal in appropriate circumstances.

5.3.3. You shall remain our employee and bound by the terms of this agreement (including any implied duties of good faith and fidelity).

5.3.4. You shall be contactable during each working day (save during periods of sickness or periods taken as holiday).

5.3.5. We may exclude you from any of our premises, and we may require you not to contact or deal with fellow employees, clients, suppliers or customers of ours.

5.6. Time spent on Garden Leave will reduce the length of post-employment restrictions set out in clause [XX], provided you have complied with the terms of your Garden Leave. This means, for example, that one month spent on Garden Leave would reduce a six-month post-termination restriction to five months.

5.7. In the event that any period of notice you give to leave your employment with the Company is greater than the period of notice you are required to give under this agreement, and we decide to put you on Garden Leave, the Company may, at its absolute discretion, treat the period of notice you give as that required under this agreement (thereby bringing forward your Termination Date).

Appendix 3

Useful template settlement agreement clauses

Important note – please read

As with the previous appendix, these template clauses are provided for general guidance only. Every situation is different, and what works for one employer or executive may not be appropriate for another.

Before using or adapting any of these clauses, you should take your own independent legal advice. Employment law and tax law can be complex, and the wording of contractual clauses may have legal or financial consequences that are not immediately obvious. You are responsible for ensuring that any clauses you use are properly drafted and tailored to your specific context.

1. Restrictive covenants

EITHER

1.1. You accept and agree that you continue to be bound by the duties and restrictions in clauses [***insert relevant clause numbers***] of your [contract of employment] [service agreement] dated [***insert date so that contract can be identified***].

OR

1.1. In consideration for the sum of £[***insert figure***], which shall be subject to appropriate PAYE deductions, you hereby agree to the restrictions set out below:

1.2. [***set out all covenants you wish to bite on the employee***]

2. Confidentiality

2.1. You accept and agree that you continue to be bound by the duties and restrictions in relation to confidentiality in clauses [***insert relevant clause numbers***] of your [contract of employment][service agreement] dated [***insert date so that contract can be identified***].

OR

Confidential Information is a defined term in the clauses below. Please amend the defined term wording as appropriate.

Confidential Information: Information in any form (including in written, oral, visual or electronic and wherever located) relating to the Company's or any Group Company's business, clients, contacts, customers, products, assets, affairs, plans or finances for the time being confidential to the Company or any Group Company and trade secrets including any know-how relating to the Company's or Group Company's business or any of its or their suppliers, clients, customers or employees, whether or not it was described as confidential or you ought to have reasonably known it was confidential.

2.2. In consideration of the payment of £[***insert figure***], which shall be subject to appropriate PAYE deductions, you agree that you will not use any Confidential Information, make or use any copies of Confidential Information in any form; or disclose any Confidential Information to any person, company or other organisation.

2.3. Nothing in this clause shall prevent you from making a protected disclosure under section 43A of the Employment Rights Act 1996.

3. Compensation payment and tax

3.1. We shall, within [14] days of the Termination Date or [14] days of the date of receipt by us of a copy of this agreement duly signed by you and your legal adviser where indicated (whichever is the later) pay to you, by way of compensation for your loss of employment, the sum of £[***insert figure***] (**Compensation Payment**).

3.2. The Company will pay the Compensation Payment less all required deductions for tax and National Insurance contributions. The parties believe the following to be correct:

3.2.1. No part of the Compensation Payment is taxable as Post-Employment Notice Pay OR The first £[insert amount] of the Compensation Payment is Post-Employment Notice Pay and is taxable as earnings. The Company shall deduct income tax and employee National Insurance contributions from it at the appropriate rate.

3.2.1. The [[next £30,000][remainder] of the] Compensation Payment will be paid tax free, as a termination award under the threshold within the meaning of sections 402A(1) and 403 of the *Income Tax (Earnings and Pensions) Act 2003*.

3.2.1. [The balance of the Compensation Payment will be taxable and we shall deduct income tax from it at the appropriate rate].

3.3. You shall be responsible for any further tax and employee's National Insurance contributions due in respect of the Compensation Payment and shall indemnify and keep indemnified the Company and any Group Company fully and effectively against all costs, claims, expenses, proceedings, penalties and interest incurred by the Company or any Group Company which arises out of or in connection with any liability to make appropriate deductions for tax or employee's National Insurance contributions in respect of the Compensation Payment.

4. Confidentiality and non-disparagement clause

Drafting note: this clause is appropriately caveated to take account of the SRA warning notice on the use of NDAs. Please note that you may wish to consider expanding sub-clause 1.5.6 (which is included to reflect the Higher Education (Freedom of Speech) Act 2023) to apply to all agreements.

Defined terms used in this clause include 'Company' and 'Group Company' – if using this wording, you should make sure that these terms are defined at the start of your agreement.

4.1. The parties agree and undertake that neither will make or publish any statement to a third party concerning this agreement, the dispute settled by it or the circumstances surrounding the termination of your employment.

4.2. The parties are able to make a comment otherwise prohibited by clause [1.1] above if they make it to:

4.2.1. In your case:

4.2.1.1. Your spouse or partner, provided they agree to keep the information confidential.

4.2.1.2. Your tax advisers or persons providing you with support services.

4.2.1.3. Your insurer.

4.2.1.4. Any government benefits agency or other organisation from which you are claiming support resulting from your loss of employment.

4.2.2. In the case of the Company:

4.2.2.1. Its officers, employees or workers.

4.2.2.2. Its legal, tax and other professional advisers.

4.3. You shall not make or publish any adverse, disparaging or derogatory comment about the Company, any Group Company or any of its or their officers, employees or workers, and you shall not do anything which shall, or may, damage or lower the reputation of the Company, any Group Company or any of its of their officers, employees or workers.

4.4. The Company or any Group Company shall not authorise or encourage any of its or their officers, employees or workers to make any adverse, disparaging or derogatory comments about you or to do or say anything which shall, or may, damage or lower your reputation.

4.5. Nothing in this clause shall prevent you, the Company or any Group Company (or any of its or their officers, employees or workers) from:

4.5.1. Reporting a suspected criminal offence to any law enforcement body.

4.5.2. Assisting with any criminal investigation or prosecution.

4.5.3. Reporting misconduct or breach of regulatory requirements to any supervising or regulatory body.

4.5.4. Co-operating with any investigation by HMRC or a regulator, ombudsman or supervising authority regarding any misconduct or wrongdoing.

4.5.5. Making any disclosure required by law.

4.5.6. [***Higher Education only*** – Reporting, discussing or publishing information regarding any complaint of bullying, harassment, sexual abuse, sexual harassment or sexual misconduct.]

4.5.7. Disclosing information about this agreement or the circumstances surrounding it to professional advisers, such as legal or tax advisors or medical professionals who are bound by a duty of confidentiality.

4.6. Nothing in this clause shall prevent you, the Company, any Group Company and any of its or their officers, employees or workers from making a protected disclosure under section 43A of the *Employment Rights Act 1996*.

4.7. You warrant that you have not done or failed to do anything prior to the date of this agreement which would be a breach of this clause if it had occurred after the date of this agreement.

Appendix 4

Draft letter of resignation from directorship

[Insert Date]

Dear [Sirs]

[Insert Company Name] (the **Company**)

I resign from my position as a director of the Company with [*immediate effect / effect from the conclusion of the board meeting at which this letter is presented*].

I confirm that I have no claim or right of action of any kind against the Company or any of its officers or employees in respect of the termination of my office or otherwise. To the extent any such claim may exist, I irrevocably waive it and release the Company, its officers and employees from all and any liability.

This letter and any dispute or claim (including non-contractual disputes or claims) arising out of or in connection with it will be governed by the law of England and Wales. The courts of England and Wales will have exclusive jurisdiction over any such dispute or claim.

Executed and delivered as a deed on the date written above.

Signed as a deed by:

____

____
[Print full name]

In the presence of:

____
Signature of Witness

Name of Witness: ______________________

Address of Witness: ______________________

Occupation of Witness: ______________________

Also by
Daniel Barnett

Preventing and DEFENDING Employee STRESS CLAIMS
Changing Terms and Conditions
HR Hazards
Model answers to 70 HR problems
Employment Tribunal COMPENSATION
Menopause and the Workplace
DANIEL BARNETT

LBC
LBC

Dear HR Professional,

I take my hat off to you.

Having supported the HR community for so many years, I know It's a challenging job you do, sometimes under really difficult circumstances.

The tricky HR issues you have to handle must take up a tremendous amount of your time, your energy and your brain power. I bet it can be exhausting for you to work under that level of pressure.

Being An HR Professional In Today's Business Environment Is TOUGH!

Maintaining your high standards of professionalism must be a real struggle, especially when your efforts and expertise often go unappreciated.

I'll wager you have to make decisions on challenging HR situations you've sometimes never encountered before. Even if you're part of a team, it must sometimes feel like you're working in isolation.

With so much complexity and ambiguity, do you ever find you're not clear whether you're doing the right thing when there's so much to think about?

I expect it can be draining too. You've got to make tough decisions which may be unpopular.

The pressure's on you to ensure people are treated fairly while the business complies with its legal obligations.

It's a thankless task, especially if you've got grief coming at you from all sides.

Doubt can creep in too. Even though you're an extremely competent professional, you might even begin to question yourself... What if you've got it wrong?

You've got to cope with all that, whilst constantly having to convince any doubting stakeholders you're adding value to the business.

That pressure must take its toll on you.

You wouldn't be human if it didn't cause you tension, stress or even worse!

Being the caring professional you are, I bet you often take work home with you.

If You're Not Careful The Stress WILL Creep Up On You

And I don't just mean opening your laptop on your couch when everyone else is watching Eastenders.

We all know of families and relationships that come a poor second to the pressures and challenges faced at work.

Yours too..?

But does it have to be that way?

Should you feel the responsibility of the HR world is entirely on your shoulders and that you've got to bear that burden alone?

The answer is a firm no.

It doesn't have to be like that.

There Is An Answer To Help Make Your Work & Your Life Much Easier For You

There's a place you can get all the help, support, advice and encouragement you need to ease the constant pressure you have to bear.

It's called the HR Inner Circle.

It will lift the burden you're carrying by giving you swift access to comprehensive resources and live practical guidance you can implement right away.

It's information I know will save you time, energy and effort.

It's a vibrant, active community of caring, like minded HR professionals willing to help you.

There are resources packed full of practical, actionable advice for you that's difficult to find anywhere else.

And it doesn't matter what you're working on.

Whether it be workforce engagement, attracting and keeping talent, diversity and inclusion or employee health and well being, you'll find support for all of that.

You're covered even if you're working on one of those tricky, sensitive, people problems you never see coming until they land squarely on your plate.

Timely Support To Make Your Job Easier, Can Be Rapidly Found In The HR Inner Circle

As a member of the HR Inner Circle, to get the support you want…

…just ask.

Your first port of call is the vibrant Facebook group, bursting at the seams with incredible HR professionals like you.

Just post your question and let it bubble and simmer in the collective genius of the group.

By the end of the day, you'll have at least 3-5 comments on your post, often more.

You'll get relevant, insightful and practical guidance that comes from the hard earned experience of your fellow members.

Often you'll get a response within a couple of hours. Sometimes you'll get an answer within minutes - even if it's late in the evening!

This highly active community never fails to astound me with just how willing they are to help fellow HR professionals like you.

They readily and generously share their hard earned knowledge and experience.

You Can Get Answers From <u>Real People</u> Quickly AND From Our Extensive Resource Library Too

> …really important for someone working on their own who needs to check things out, or just bounce a few ideas around.
>
> - Quentin Colborn
> Director, QC People Management Ltd

While you wait for a response from the Facebook group, you'll likely find answers in the resource-rich members' vault on our secure online portal as well.

It takes just 2 clicks and a quick keyword search using our Rapid Results Search Tool.

You'll instantly find precisely where your topic is covered in our extensive back catalogue of monthly magazines and audio seminars.

In under 30 seconds you can find exactly what you're after.

It's that quick and easy.

...And if you need a specific legal insight?

Then pose your question live to an expert employment lawyer in our monthly Q&A session.

It'll either be me or one of my prominent contemporaries. You'll get your answer immediately without having to pay any legal costs.

If you can't wait, you'll find where it's been answered before with a quick search of previous Q&A sessions.

Our clever index system means you can find a question, and in a single click get straight to the recorded answer.

But perhaps you need to dive deep and explore the different options open to you to solve a particularly tricky problem?

Then join one of our monthly HR Huddles. There you can run your specific situation past other HR professionals.

They'll offer their insights, share their experience and work WITH you to find a solution that works FOR you.

You'll find all of this in one convenient place - the HR Inner Circle.

It's Been A Labour Of Love Putting The HR Inner Circle Together So It Works For Professionals Like You

> **It's great to see that we all experience tricky cases from time to time.**
>
> - Annabelle Carey
> Managing Consultant, HR Services Partnership

I've spent years practising law and have become recognised as one of the UK's leading employment law barristers. I've even got my own radio show!

But more importantly for you, I've also developed another skill.

It's bringing useful employment expertise AND practical experience together in a way that supports busy, overworked (and sometimes stressed) HR professionals like you.

Everything you're likely to need is **literally at your fingertips**.

This will save you **time, energy** and **effort.**

Being a member also means your business and clients will see you as even MORE INFORMED about the intricacies of employment law.

They'll marvel at how well you keep up to date when you're busy working so hard for them.

You'll be seen making quicker decisions and implementing effective solutions to accelerate the growth of the organisation.

You'll make impressive time and cost savings for the business.

And those tricky, off-piste situations you've never come across before..?

Well, nothing will faze you, because you're backed up by an HR support system second to none.

But more importantly, you'll feel that pressure gently ease off.

With the relief you'll feel knowing that such great help and guidance is just a few minutes, you'll wonder how you survived without it!

That's Why I'm Inviting You To Join And Reap The Many Rewards Of Membership

WWW.HRINNERCIRCLE.CO.UK

Here's what you get when you join the HR Inner Circle:

Benefit #1- you'll get unlimited access to the hugely popular HR Inner Circle Facebook Private Group

- Tap into the vast wealth of knowledge, experience, insight and wisdom of the top 0.5% of your profession at any time, day or night.
- In less than 5 minutes you can post ANY HR question and get insightful answers and suggestions in a couple of hours or less, from some of the best in your profession.
- Fast track your impact by discovering effective shortcuts and workarounds from HR people who've been "there" and done "it".
- Expand and deepen your network of like minded individuals, secure in the knowledge they're as dedicated and as ambitious as you.

- Increase your prestige with your colleagues and stakeholders by being part of such an exclusive and prominent HR community.
- Gain confidence in your judgment and decisions by using the highly responsive community as a sounding board for your ideas.

Benefit #2 - you'll receive 11 copies of the HR Inner Circular Magazine every year

- Enjoy that satisfying "THUD" on your door mat every month when the postman delivers your very own copy of the HR Inner Circular magazine.
- Quickly discover exactly what the law says about key issues affecting HR professionals around the UK like you.
- Get concise and practical guidance on how employment law applies to the challenging situations and circumstances you deal with every day.
- Avoid the mistakes of others by applying the lessons from the in depth analysis of real life case studies.
- Benefit from a legal deep dive by the UK's leading employment law barrister into a topical employment question posed by a fellow member (perhaps you!).
- Review a summary of recent important Facebook Group discussions worthy of sharing, that you may have missed.
- Explore a range of related and relevant topics useful for your practice and your broader professional development.

The magazine is really informative, the Facebook group such a community, and I think exceptional value for money.

- Lis Moore
Head of Advisory & Support Services,
Society of Local Council Clerks

Benefit #3 - Monthly Audio Seminars

- A 60 minute legal deep dive by me into an important subject relevant to you and your practice.
- Professionally recorded content recorded exclusively for the HR Inner Circle - you'll not find this information anywhere else.
- Carefully structured content that's easy to consume, understand and apply in your work as an HR professional.
- Episodes delivered every month so you can stay current on the latest issues affecting HR professionals.
- The convenience of listening to the recording online or downloading the mp3 for later enjoyment at a time suitable to your busy schedule (perfect for any commute).

Benefit #4 - you get an exclusive invite to a live online Q&A Session every fortnight, led by an expert employment lawyer

- Gain 60 minutes of live and direct access to the sharpest legal minds from my secret little black book of contacts.
- Get answers to your knottiest employment law questions, and solutions to your trickiest HR problems, from some of the brightest employment lawyers in the UK.
- Avoid having to pay the £300-£400 it would cost you to ask a lawyer your question outside of the HR Inner Circle.
- Benefit from valuable insights from the answers given to other members.
- If you can't attend live, watch the recording when it's convenient for you.
- Quickly access the recorded answer to any question asked in the session by simply clicking the question index for that session.

- Save time by downloading the session transcription to scan-read at a time suitable for you.

Benefit #5 - join a live Monthly Huddle with other HR Professionals to solve your most challenging HR problems

- Attend your very own mini-mastermind group of highly qualified, highly regarded and experienced fellow HR professionals to "group think" through an issue you're facing right now.
- Develop bespoke solutions to the unique problems and challenges you have to deal with in a safe, supportive and confidential environment.
- Feel safe knowing these online zoom calls are NOT recorded to respect the sensitivity of issues addressed and the privacy of those involved. [NOTE - a professional transcriber attends and takes written notes. An anonymised summary is then made available to the membership]
- Recent Huddle topics included changing employee benefits, mandatory vaccination, career breaks, sickness during disciplinaries, effective worker forums and hybrid working arrangements.

Benefit #6 - access our Templates & Resources Centre

- Gain immediate access to our library of the most popular and frequently used forms, assessments, agreements, checklists, letter templates, questionnaires and reports to help the busiest HR professionals save time and get things done quicker and easier.
- Download them as Word documents, so you can edit and personalise them to fit your business needs
- New templates added every single month

Benefit #7 - build your own Employment Law Library

- We send you several brand-new books on employment law several times each year
- Acquire your own physical library of concise, easy-to-read and fully updated textbooks
- Recent titles include Hiring Staff, Managing Sickness Absence, Spotting Malingering and Resolving Grievances

Benefit #8 - free Ticket to our Annual Conference

- The perfect opportunity to extend your personal network of fellow HR professionals.
- Meet up face to face with the people who've been supporting you in the Facebook Group and HR Huddles so you can deepen those connections even further.
- Gather key insights and takeaways to help you personally and professionally from some of the best speakers on the circuit. Previous speakers have covered motivation, dealing with difficult people, goal setting and productivity, decision making and social media marketing.
- Get instant access to recordings of all previous conferences so even if you can't attend in person, you can benefit from the event in your own time.
- Includes probably the best conference lunch you'll ever have - a bold claim I know, but we use outstanding caterers.

It never ceases to amaze me the amount of time and effort people put into the Facebook group, sharing their experiences, advice, and sage words of wisdom.

- Emma Lister
HR Consultant, SME HR Services

Benefit #9 - your Personal Concierge will help you get the best out of your membership

- You get personal access to Nina who'll point you in the direction of exactly where to find what you need. She's supported hundreds of members over the 5 years she's been part of the team.
- Nina also works closely with the 11 back office staff that support the operation. In the extremely unlikely event she doesn't know where something is, she knows who will.

HOW MUCH DOES JOINING THE HR INNER CIRCLE COST?

There's no doubt in my mind the annual value of membership benefits is in the many thousands of pounds range.

But you're not going to pay anywhere near that.

Let me remind you of what that small monthly fee gives you every year

Access to the private Facebook Group	INCLUDED
HR Inner Circular Magazine subscription	INCLUDED
Monthly Audio Seminars	INCLUDED
Live Q&A sessions	INCLUDED
Monthly HR Huddles	INCLUDED
Templates & Resources Centre	INCLUDED
Employment Law Library	INCLUDED
Free ticket to the HR Inner Circle Annual Conference	INCLUDED
Your Personal Membership Concierge	INCLUDED

TOTAL PRICELESS

Another way of looking at your investment is this:

Because access to what you need is so quick…

Join today and that price is fixed for as long as you remain a member. You'll always pay the same, even if we increase the price to new members (which we regularly do).

…it's like having your very own part time, legally trained, assistant HR Business Partner, just waiting to provide you with all the answers you need…

WWW.HRINNERCIRCLE.CO.UK

Plus, With Membership Of The HR Inner Circle, You'll Also Get These 4 Additional Resources For FREE!

Additional Resource #1 - Handling Awkward Conversations

A video case study masterclass you can share with managers to train them to handle awkward staff disciplinary, performance and attitude problems. A huge time saver for you.

Additional Resource #2 - 6 x HR Employment Online Courses

Immediate, on demand access to six thorough, online HR courses (with more constantly added), including Employment Tribunal Compensation, Chat GPT for HR Professionals, Deconstructing TUPE, Changing Terms & Conditions, Unconscious Bias At Work and Handling Grievances.

Additional Resource #3 - Free listing on the Register of Investigators

Advertise your professional investigations service in our member's portal.

Additional Resource #4 - Significant discounts on sets of policies, contracts, and other courses.

Get member discounts on my Getting Redundancy Right and HR Policies products as well as other price reductions as new products are released.

> It's a really good investment. The support you get from other Facebook group members is fantastic. Whatever your question, someone will know the answer. Access to Daniel's experience and knowledge through the podcasts and Q&A is invaluable too.
>
> - Tracy Madgwick
> HR Consultant, Crafnant HR

I'm So Confident Joining The HR Inner Circle Is The Right Decision For You, Here's My

NO LIMITS GUARANTEE

Take action and join the HR Inner Circle **now**.

If you're not 100% satisfied with your investment, you can cancel at ANY time.

Just tell us, and your membership will end immediately. No long-term contracts. No notice periods. No fuss.

I'm comfortable doing this because I know once you join, you'll find the support, the information and the strategies so useful, you'll never want to leave.

Before you decide though, let me be very clear about membership of the HR Inner Circle.

It's only for ambitious and dedicated HR professionals who want to accelerate and increase their impact by plugging into an HR ecosystem with its finger firmly on the pulse of what's working right now in HR.

If you're just plodding along and are content with just getting by, then this is probably not for you.

But if you're drawn to benefiting from standing shoulder to shoulder with some of the giants in the HR community who will help you solve your toughest problems, then joining the HR Inner Circle is the RIGHT decision for you.

Join here now:

WWW.HRINNERCIRCLE.CO.UK

Daniel Barnett

P.S. Remember when you join you get unrestricted access to the private Facebook group, the monthly magazine delivered direct to your door, the monthly audio seminar, regular free books, templates, checklists and resources, on-demand video courses, over 100 audio seminars and back copies of magazines, live interactive Q&A sessions with a lawyer, focused monthly huddles with other HR professionals, a free ticket to the annual conference, your personal concierge plus a bunch of additional resources…